PARENTING

FROM HOME TO CLASSROOM

PARENTING TIPS FOR A SUCCESFUL SCHOOL TRANSITION

ALI YILDIRIM

Published by Omega IP Holding, Inc.
Philadelphia, PA, United States
https://www.morzaik.us
ISBN: 978-1-970277-62-3
(Morzaik Publishing by Omega IP Holding, Inc)

Printed in the United States of America

Cover design & Illustrations by
Morzaik Publishing
First Edition – 2025

Table Of Contents

Preface

There is a particular kind of quiet that fills a house on the morning of a child's first day of school. It is the quiet of a threshold — something is ending, and something new is beginning. For children, that threshold can feel enormous. For parents, it can feel even larger.

This book was written for that moment, and for all the moments that surround it.

The transition from home to classroom is far more than a logistical shift in schedules and school bags. It is an emotional passage — for the child learning to navigate a world beyond the safety of home, and for the parent watching them take their first independent steps into it. It can bring out the best in a family: tenderness, creativity, patience, and love. But it can also surface fears and anxieties that no parenting manual ever quite prepares you for.

From Home to Classroom was written because that preparation matters deeply. Research consistently shows that children who transition smoothly into school — who feel emotionally secure, adequately prepared, and genuinely supported — go on to develop stronger academic habits, healthier social relationships, and greater resilience in the face of life's challenges. The early weeks and months of school don't just shape a child's first year — they shape how a child thinks about learning itself.

Throughout these chapters, you will find practical strategies grounded in both child development research and the lived reality of parenting. You will find advice on reading your child's emotional cues, building their confidence before school even begins, establishing routines that calm rather than create chaos, and forming a meaningful partnership with the teachers and staff who will become an extension of your child's support network.

You will also find honesty — because this transition is not always smooth, and that is okay. Every child is different. Every family is different. What works beautifully for one child may need to be adapted entirely for another. This book does not offer a single perfect formula; it offers a toolkit, and the encouragement to trust your own instincts as a parent.

More than anything, this book is a reminder that your presence — your attention, your reassurance, your willingness to show up — is the most powerful tool you have. Children don't need perfect parents. They need present ones.

So take a breath. Turn the page. And know that by simply picking up this book, you have already taken the most important step of all.

Ali Yildirim

Chapter 1: Understanding the Importance of a Smooth School Transition

The impact of a successful school transition on a child's academic and emotional development

Starting school is a massive shift for a child, not just academically, but emotionally. When kids feel secure stepping from their living room into a classroom, it lays the groundwork for how they view education for years to come. Instead of just surviving the day, a smooth transition helps them build the confidence to actually absorb what they are being taught. They learn to self-regulate when things get frustrating, making it easier to forge friendships and embrace the messiness of growing up.

Academic success is closely linked to a child's ability to adjust to the school environment. When a child transitions smoothly into school, they are more likely to feel comfortable in their new surroundings and be able to focus on learning. This can lead to improved academic performance and a greater sense of accomplishment. Additionally, children who have a positive school transition are more likely to develop strong study habits and a love for learning that will serve them well throughout their academic career.

Emotionally, a successful school transition can have a profound impact on a child's development. Children who transition smoothly into school are more likely to feel secure and supported, which can lead to higher levels of self-esteem and emotional well-being. They are also more likely to develop strong social relationships with their peers, which can help them navigate the challenges of growing up and forming healthy relationships. Overall, a successful school transition can set the stage for a child to develop the emotional resilience and coping skills needed to thrive in school and beyond.

Parenting plays a crucial role in easing a child's school transition and setting them up for success. By providing emotional support, encouragement, and guidance, parents can help their child feel confident and prepared for the challenges of school. It is important for parents to communicate openly with their child about their feelings and concerns, and to provide reassurance and support as needed.

Additionally, parents can help their child develop positive coping strategies, such as deep breathing exercises or journaling, to manage any anxiety or stress that may arise during the school transition process.

In conclusion, the impact of a successful school transition on a child's academic and emotional development is significant. By fostering a smooth transition from home to the classroom, parents can help their child build a strong foundation for academic success and emotional well-being. Through open communication, emotional support, and positive parenting strategies, parents can ease their child's transition into school and set them up for a positive and fulfilling educational experience.

Common challenges children face during the school transition period

The transition period from home to school can be a challenging time for children as they navigate a new environment, routine, and social dynamics. There are several common challenges that children may face during this time, and it is important for parents to be aware of them in order to support their child through the transition.

One common challenge that children may face during the school transition period is separation anxiety. Leaving the familiar environment of home and being apart from parents can be a daunting experience for many children, especially those who are starting school for the first time. It is important for parents to acknowledge and validate their child's feelings of anxiety, while also providing reassurance and support to help them feel more secure and confident in their new surroundings.

Another challenge that children may face during the school transition period is adjusting to a new routine. The structured schedule of the school day can be a significant change from the more flexible routine of home life, and children may struggle to adapt to the expectations and demands of the school day. Parents can help their child by establishing a consistent routine at home that mirrors the school schedule, and by providing plenty of opportunities for their child to practice and develop the skills needed to succeed in a school setting.

Social challenges are also common during the school transition period, as children navigate new friendships, peer relationships, and social dynamics. Some children may feel shy, anxious, or overwhelmed in social situations, while others may struggle to make connections with their peers. Parents can support their child by helping them develop social skills, encouraging them to participate in social activities, and fostering a positive and inclusive attitude towards others.

Academic challenges can also arise during the school transition period, as children adjust to the expectations and demands of the classroom environment. Some children may find it difficult to focus, stay organized, or keep up with the pace of the curriculum, leading to feelings of frustration, anxiety, or inadequacy. Parents can support their child by providing a quiet and organized study space at home, helping them with homework and assignments, and communicating regularly with teachers to address any concerns or challenges that may arise.

Overall, the school transition period can be a time of significant change and adjustment for children, as they navigate new environments, routines, and social dynamics. By being aware of the common challenges that children may face during this time, parents can provide the support, guidance, and reassurance that their child needs to thrive and succeed in the school setting. With patience, understanding, and empathy, parents can help their child navigate the school transition period with confidence and resilience.

The role of parents in facilitating a smooth transition from home to classroom

The transition from home to classroom can be a challenging time for both children and parents. As a parent, your role in facilitating a smooth transition for your child is crucial in ensuring their success in school. In this subchapter, we will discuss the important role parents play in helping their children adjust to the new environment of school.

One of the key ways parents can help their child transition from home to classroom is by providing emotional support. Starting school can be an overwhelming experience for young children, and it is important for parents to reassure them that they are loved and supported. By creating a safe and nurturing environment at home, children will feel more confident and secure as they embark on this new chapter in their lives.

Another important aspect of preparing your child for school is to establish a routine. Children thrive on structure and predictability, so it is essential for parents to create a daily schedule that includes time for homework, play, and rest. By setting clear expectations and boundaries, children will know what to expect each day and feel more prepared for the school environment.

Parenting strategies for easing school transition also include involving your child in the decision-making process. By allowing your child to have a say in choosing their school supplies, backpack, and lunch options, they will feel more empowered and excited about starting school. Additionally, parents can help ease the transition by talking to their child about what to expect in the classroom and answering any questions they may have.

Ultimately, the role of parents in facilitating a smooth transition from home to classroom is vital in helping children adjust to the new school environment. By providing emotional support, establishing routines, and involving your child in the decision-making process, parents can help ease the transition and set their child up for success in school. Remember, starting school is a big step for both children and parents, but with the right support and guidance, the transition can be a positive and rewarding experience for the whole family.

Chapter 2:
Preparing Your Child Emotionally for Starting School

Recognizing signs of anxiety or fear in your child about starting school

Recognizing signs of anxiety or fear in your child about starting school is an important aspect of helping them transition successfully. Children may exhibit various symptoms of anxiety or fear when faced with the prospect of starting school, and it is crucial for parents to be able to identify these signs in order to provide the necessary support and reassurance. By being aware of these indicators, parents can take proactive steps to help their child navigate the transition with confidence and ease.

One common sign of anxiety or fear in children about starting school is changes in behavior. This may manifest as increased clinginess, irritability, or withdrawal from social interactions. Children may also exhibit physical symptoms such as headaches, stomachaches, or difficulty sleeping. It is important for parents to pay attention to these changes and address any concerns with their child in a supportive and understanding manner.

Another indicator of anxiety or fear in children about starting school is expressed through verbal cues. Children may voice concerns about making friends, being away from their parents, or not understanding the school work. It is important for parents to listen to their child's worries and validate their feelings. By acknowledging their concerns, parents can help their child feel heard and supported as they prepare for this new chapter in their lives.

Additionally, children may display signs of anxiety or fear through their body language. This can include fidgeting, avoiding eye contact, or seeking reassurance from their parents. By observing these nonverbal cues, parents can gain insight into their child's emotional state and provide the necessary comfort and encouragement. It is important for parents to create a safe and nurturing environment where their child feels comfortable expressing their feelings and fears about starting school.

In conclusion, recognizing signs of anxiety or fear in your child about starting school is essential for helping them transition successfully. By being attuned to changes in behavior, verbal cues, and body language, parents can provide the necessary support and reassurance to help their child navigate this important milestone with confidence and ease. By addressing their concerns and fears in a loving and understanding manner, parents can help their child feel prepared and empowered as they embark on this new chapter in their educational journey.

Building your child's confidence and self-esteem before the school transition

A child's self-esteem is their emotional armor. Before they even step foot in the school, you can help them build that armor by focusing on their effort rather than just their natural talents. If they are struggling to tie their shoes or finish a puzzle, resist the urge to jump in and do it for them. Let them wrestle with the problem, and praise their persistence. When kids learn that it's okay to find things difficult and that pushing through is something to be proud of, they are much less likely to crumble when they encounter a tough math problem or a tricky social situation at recess.

One way to build your child's confidence before the school transition is to praise their efforts and accomplishments. Encouraging your child and acknowledging their achievements, no matter how small, can help boost their self-esteem and make them feel more confident in their abilities. By focusing on the positive aspects of your child's behavior and actions, you can help them develop a strong sense of self-worth that will carry over into the school setting.

Another important aspect of building your child's confidence and self-esteem before the school transition is to provide opportunities for them to socialize and interact with other children. Playdates, extracurricular activities, and community events can all help your child develop social skills and build relationships with their peers. By encouraging your child to engage in social activities, you can help them feel more comfortable and confident in social settings, which will be beneficial when they start school.

It is also important to communicate openly with your child about their feelings and concerns regarding the school transition. Encourage them to express their emotions and listen attentively to their thoughts and worries. By validating your child's feelings and providing reassurance and support, you can help them feel more confident and secure as they prepare for this new experience.

In conclusion, building your child's confidence and self-esteem before the school transition is essential for their emotional well-being and success in the classroom. By praising their efforts, providing opportunities for socialization, and communicating openly with them, you can help your child feel more prepared and confident as they embark on this new chapter in their lives. Remember that every child is unique, so it is important to tailor your approach to suit your child's individual needs and personality. With your support and guidance, your child will be well-equipped to navigate the school transition with confidence and ease.

Teaching your child coping strategies for managing emotions during the transition period

Transitioning from home to the classroom can be a challenging time for both children and parents. It is normal for children to experience a range of emotions during this period, including anxiety, excitement, and fear. As parents, it is important to teach your child coping strategies to help manage these emotions effectively.

One key strategy for helping your child manage their emotions during the transition period is to encourage open communication. Create a safe space for your child to express how they are feeling and validate their emotions. Let them know that it is okay to feel nervous or scared about starting school, and reassure them that you are there to support them through this transition.

Another important coping strategy is to help your child develop a routine. Establishing a consistent daily schedule can provide structure and predictability, which can help reduce anxiety and stress. Encourage your child to participate in creating their own routine, including activities such as bedtime rituals, meal times, and study periods.

Teaching your child relaxation techniques can also be beneficial in managing emotions during the transition period. Practice deep breathing exercises, mindfulness, or progressive muscle relaxation with your child to help them calm down when they are feeling overwhelmed. These techniques can be useful tools for managing stress and anxiety in a variety of situations.

Lastly, encourage your child to engage in activities that promote emotional well-being, such as exercise, art, music, or spending time outdoors. These activities can help your child release pent-up emotions and improve their overall mood. By teaching your child coping strategies for managing emotions during the transition period, you can help them navigate this challenging time with confidence and resilience.

Chapter 3: Parenting Strategies for Easing School Transition

Establishing a routine to help your child adjust to the school schedule

Kids are creatures of habit who crave predictability; it makes their world feel safe. If mornings are a chaotic scramble of searching for shoes and rushing through breakfast, that frantic energy follows them right to their desk. Try walking the routine backward from the time you need to leave the house. Build in a buffer of fifteen extra minutes, lay out clothes the night before, and keep a visual checklist on the fridge. When mornings run on a calm, predictable track, children arrive at school ready to learn rather than exhausted from the commute.

One way to establish a routine is to set a consistent bedtime and wake-up time for your child. Getting enough sleep is crucial for a child's physical and emotional well-being, so it's important to ensure they are well-rested for the school day. By sticking to a regular sleep schedule, you can help your child adjust to the early mornings and long days of school.

In addition to setting a bedtime and wake-up time, it's also helpful to create a morning routine that your child can follow each day. This might include tasks such as getting dressed, eating breakfast, and packing their school bag. By having a set routine in the morning, you can help your child feel more organized and prepared for the day ahead.

Another important aspect of establishing a routine is scheduling regular meal times for your child. Eating at consistent times can help regulate your child's energy levels and keep them focused throughout the school day. Providing nutritious meals and snacks can also support your child's physical and mental well-being as they adjust to the demands of school.

Overall, creating a routine for your child can help them feel more secure and confident as they transition to the school schedule. By setting consistent bedtimes, morning routines, and meal times, you can provide your child with the structure and support they need to succeed in school. With a solid routine in place, your child will be better equipped to handle the challenges of the school day and thrive in their new environment.

Communicating effectively with teachers and school staff to support your child's transition

Communication between parents and teachers is crucial in supporting a child's successful transition from home to the classroom. By establishing open lines of communication, parents can work together with school staff to ensure that their child's needs are met and that they are supported in their new environment. This subchapter will provide valuable tips and strategies for effectively communicating with teachers and school staff to support your child during this important time.

One key tip for effective communication with teachers and school staff is to establish a positive and collaborative relationship from the start. This means being proactive in reaching out to teachers, attending school meetings and events, and showing a willingness to work together to support your child's transition. By demonstrating a positive and collaborative attitude, parents can help to build trust and rapport with teachers, which can lead to more effective communication and support for their child.

Another important aspect of effective communication with teachers and school staff is to be clear and specific about your child's needs and concerns. This may involve sharing information about your child's strengths, challenges, and any special accommodations or support they may require. By providing teachers with this information, parents can help to ensure that their child receives the necessary support and resources to thrive in the classroom.

It is also important for parents to actively listen to teachers and school staff and to take their feedback and suggestions into consideration. Teachers are professionals with valuable insights and expertise, and by listening to their feedback and advice, parents can gain a better understanding of how to support their child's transition. By working together with teachers in a collaborative and respectful manner, parents can help to create a positive and supportive environment for their child at school.

In conclusion, effective communication with teachers and school staff is essential in supporting your child's successful transition from home to the classroom. By establishing a positive and collaborative relationship, being clear and specific about your child's needs, and actively listening to teachers and school staff, parents can work together with educators to ensure that their child receives the necessary support and resources to thrive in the school environment. By following these tips and strategies, parents can help to ease their child's transition and set them up for success in school.

Creating a supportive home environment that encourages learning and academic success

A home that values learning doesn't necessarily mean one covered in flashcards and educational posters. It's about cultivating an atmosphere where curiosity is celebrated. Create a dedicated, clutter-free spot for homework, even if it's just a specific corner of the kitchen table with a caddy of supplies. More importantly, show a genuine interest in their day that goes beyond asking, "How was school?" Try asking,

"What was the funniest thing that happened today?" or "Did anything surprise you?" This shows them that you value their daily experiences, not just the grades on their report card.

One way to create a supportive home environment is to establish a routine that includes dedicated time for homework and study. Setting aside a specific time each day for academic activities will not only help your child stay organized but also instill a sense of discipline and responsibility. By creating a consistent study routine, you are showing your child the importance of prioritizing their education and fostering good study habits.

In addition to establishing a study routine, it is important to create a designated study space in your home. This could be a quiet corner in the living room, a desk in their bedroom, or any other area where your child can focus and concentrate without distractions. Providing them with a comfortable and well- equipped study area will help them stay focused and engaged in their schoolwork, ultimately leading to better academic performance.

Furthermore, it is essential to show interest in your

child's academic progress and be actively involved in their learning journey. Take the time to review their homework, ask about their day at school, and engage in conversations about what they are learning. By showing genuine interest and support for their education, you are reinforcing the value of learning and encouraging them to excel in their studies.

Lastly, creating a supportive home environment also involves fostering a positive attitude towards learning and academic success. Encourage your child to set goals, celebrate their achievements, and embrace challenges as opportunities for growth. By promoting a growth mindset and emphasizing the importance of perseverance and hard work, you are helping your child develop the resilience and determination needed to succeed in school and beyond.

Chapter 4: Building a Strong Parent-School Partnership

The benefits of collaborating with your child's school to support their transition

Collaborating with your child's school to support their transition can have numerous benefits for both you and your child. By working together with teachers and school administrators, you can ensure that your child's transition from home to the classroom is as smooth and successful as possible. This collaboration can help to ease any anxieties or fears your child may have about starting school, and can also help to establish a strong foundation for their academic and social success.

One of the key benefits of collaborating with your child's school is that it can help to create a sense of continuity and consistency for your child. When parents and teachers are on the same page and working together towards a common goal, children are more likely to feel supported and secure in their new environment. This can help to reduce any feelings of anxiety or uncertainty that your child may have about starting school, and can help to establish a positive and supportive relationship between your family and the school.

Another benefit of collaborating with your child's school is that it can help to ensure that your child's individual needs and preferences are taken into account during their transition. By communicating openly with teachers and school administrators, you can provide valuable insights into your child's personality, learning style, and interests. This information can help teachers to better understand and support your child, and can help to tailor their transition plan to meet your child's unique needs.

Collaborating with your child's school can also help to foster a sense of community and belonging for your family. By actively participating in school events, volunteering in the classroom, and building relationships with teachers and other parents, you can help to create a supportive network of individuals who are invested in your child's success. This sense of community can provide valuable emotional support for both you and your child during the transition process, and can help to create a positive and welcoming school environment for your family.

Overall, collaborating with your child's school to support their transition can have a range of benefits for both you and your child. By working together with teachers and school administrators, you can help to create a smooth and successful transition from home to the classroom, establish a sense of continuity and consistency for your child, ensure their individual needs are met, and foster a sense of community and belonging for your family. By taking an active role in your child's school transition, you can help to set them up for academic and social success in the years to come.

Tips for fostering positive relationships with teachers and school administrators

Think of your child's teacher as a partner, not just a service provider. Building a strong relationship with them early in the year prevents minor hiccups from turning into major roadblocks. You don't need to send daily emails, but a quick note at the start of the term introducing your child's quirks—like how they get shy in loud groups or need a minute to transition between tasks—gives the teacher a massive head start. If an issue does pop up, approach it with curiosity rather than defensiveness, asking, "What are you seeing in the classroom, and how can we mirror your strategies at home?"

One tip for fostering positive relationships with teachers and school administrators is to communicate openly and effectively. Keep the lines of communication open by attending parent-teacher conferences, volunteering in the classroom, and staying informed about your child's progress. By communicating regularly with teachers and school administrators, you can address any concerns or issues that may arise and work together to find solutions.

Another tip is to show appreciation for the hard work and dedication of teachers and school administrators. A simple thank you note or gesture of gratitude can go a long way in building positive relationships. Acknowledge the efforts of these individuals in helping your child learn and grow, and express your gratitude for their support and guidance.

Additionally, it is important to be respectful and considerate in your interactions with teachers and school administrators. Treat them with kindness and professionalism, and show understanding and empathy for the challenges they may face in their roles. By demonstrating respect and consideration, you can build trust and rapport with these individuals and create a positive and supportive school environment for your child.

Lastly, be proactive in seeking out opportunities to collaborate with teachers and school administrators. Offer to assist with classroom activities, participate in school events, and engage in discussions about your child's education. By actively engaging with teachers and school administrators, you can build strong relationships based on mutual respect and cooperation, and work together to support your child's successful transition from home to the classroom.

Advocating for your child's needs and concerns during the school transition process

Advocating for your child's needs and concerns during the school transition process is a crucial aspect of ensuring a successful start to their academic journey. As a parent, you play a key role in advocating for your child and ensuring that their individual needs are met during this important transition period. By being proactive and assertive in communicating with teachers, administrators, and other school staff, you can help create a supportive environment where your child can thrive.

One of the first steps in advocating for your child's needs during the school transition process is to familiarize yourself with their individual strengths, weaknesses, and preferences. Take the time to meet with your child's teachers and discuss any concerns or special accommodations that may be needed. By sharing this information with school staff, you can help ensure that your child receives the support they need to succeed in the classroom.

In addition to meeting with teachers, it's important to stay informed about your child's progress and well-being at school. Attend parent-teacher conferences, school events, and other opportunities to connect with school staff and stay updated on your child's academic and social development. By staying actively involved in your child's education, you can better advocate for their needs and address any concerns that may arise during the school transition process.

Another important aspect of advocating for your child's needs during the school transition process is to be prepared to address any challenges or obstacles that may arise. If your child is struggling with a particular subject or adjustment to the school environment, don't hesitate to seek out additional support or resources. By working together with school staff and other professionals, you can help identify solutions and develop strategies to help your child overcome any obstacles they may face.

Overall, advocating for your child's needs and concerns during the school transition process is a proactive and essential part of parenting. By being informed, involved, and assertive in advocating for your child, you can help create a positive and supportive environment where they can thrive academically and socially. Remember that you are your child's greatest advocate, and by working together with school staff and other professionals, you can help ensure a successful start to their academic journey.

Chapter 5: Nurturing a Love for Learning in Your Child

Encouraging curiosity and a growth mindset in your child

The way we talk about mistakes shapes how our kids view failure. If they hear us groan about a mistake we made at work or see us give up on a complicated recipe, they internalize the idea that failure is something to be ashamed of. To nurture a growth mindset, normalize the struggle. Try using the word "yet" when they get frustrated. If they say, "I can't read this," gently correct them with, "You can't read this *yet*." This tiny linguistic shift reframes a dead-end into a detour, showing them that learning is an ongoing process of leveling up.

One way to encourage curiosity in your child is to provide them with a variety of stimulating experiences and opportunities for exploration. This could involve taking them on nature walks, visiting museums, or simply engaging them in conversations about the world around them. By exposing your child to new ideas and experiences, you can help spark their curiosity and encourage them to ask questions and seek out answers.

In addition to fostering curiosity, it is important to instill a growth mindset in your child. This means teaching them that their abilities and intelligence are not fixed, but can be developed through hard work and perseverance. Encourage your child to view challenges as opportunities for growth and learning, rather than obstacles to be avoided. By praising their effort and persistence, rather than just their achievements, you can help build their confidence and resilience.

It is also important to model a growth mindset for your child by demonstrating a willingness to learn and grow yourself. Show them that you are not afraid to try new things or make mistakes, and emphasize the importance of continuous learning and improvement. By setting a positive example, you can inspire your child to adopt a similar attitude towards their own learning and development.

By encouraging curiosity and a growth mindset in your child, you are laying the foundation for their success in school and beyond. By fostering these qualities from a young age, you can help your child develop a love of learning, resilience in the face of challenges, and a willingness to embrace new opportunities. With your support and guidance, your child can approach school with confidence and enthusiasm, ready to take on whatever challenges come their way.

Providing opportunities for hands-on learning and exploration outside of the classroom

The classroom is just one place where education happens. Often, the concepts that stick best are the ones kids can touch, smell, and experience in the real world. You don't need to plan elaborate, expensive field trips to make this happen. Let them help you double a recipe in the kitchen to practice fractions, or take a walk around the neighborhood and see how many different types of leaves they can identify. Connecting what they are learning on a whiteboard to the physical world around them makes the curriculum click in a way that reading a textbook simply cannot.

One way to provide opportunities for hands-on learning is to take your child on field trips to museums, science centers, and other educational venues. These outings not only expose children to new ideas and concepts but also allow them to see how these concepts are applied in the real world. For example, a trip to a science museum can help reinforce the principles of physics, chemistry, and biology that your child is learning in school. Similarly, a visit to a historical site can bring history lessons to life and make them more meaningful and memorable.

Another way to encourage hands-on learning is to engage your child in practical activities at home. For example, you can involve them in cooking meals, gardening, or completing DIY projects around the house. These activities not only teach valuable life skills but also reinforce academic concepts such as measurement, geometry, and problem-solving. By incorporating hands-on learning opportunities into your daily routine, you can make learning more engaging and enjoyable for your child.

Outdoor exploration is another excellent way to provide hands-on learning experiences for your child. By taking nature walks, going on hikes, or visiting parks and playgrounds, you can help your child develop a greater appreciation for the world around them. Outdoor exploration also provides opportunities for children to engage in physical activity, which is essential for their overall health and well-being. Encouraging your child to explore the outdoors can help them develop a sense of curiosity, wonder, and appreciation for the natural world.

In conclusion, providing opportunities for hands-on learning and exploration outside of the classroom is crucial for your child's development and academic success. By engaging in activities that allow them to apply their knowledge in real-world settings, you can help your child develop a deeper understanding of the concepts they are learning in school. Whether through field trips, practical activities at home, or outdoor exploration, hands-on learning experiences can enrich your child's education and make learning more meaningful and enjoyable. As parents, it is important to prioritize these opportunities and support your child's curiosity and love of learning.

Celebrating your child's achievements and milestones throughout their school journey

In the rush of daily life, it is easy to let small victories slip by unnoticed. Celebrating milestones shouldn't just be reserved for graduation days or straight-A report cards. Notice the micro-wins: the first time they remember to pack their own backpack without being asked, or the day they finally read a whole sentence without stumbling. You don't need to buy them a toy every time they succeed; a spontaneous living room dance party, choosing the dinner menu, or simply looking them in the eye and saying, "I noticed how hard you worked on that, and I'm really proud of you," reinforces their internal drive to keep trying.

One way to celebrate your child's achievements is to create a special ritual or tradition that is unique to your family. This could be something as simple as going out for ice cream after a good report card, or having a family movie night to celebrate the end of a successful school year. By creating these special moments, you are creating memories that your child will cherish for years to come.

It is also important to involve your child in the celebration of their achievements. By allowing them to have a say in how they would like to celebrate, you are empowering them to take ownership of their accomplishments. This can help to boost their self-esteem and sense of independence, as they see the direct correlation between their hard work and the rewards that come with it.

Another way to celebrate your child's achievements is to display their work or awards in a prominent place in your home. This can serve as a constant reminder of their successes and can help to motivate them to continue to work hard and achieve their goals. Additionally, sharing their achievements with friends and family can also be a source of pride and encouragement for your child.

In conclusion, celebrating your child's achievements and milestones throughout their school journey is essential for their growth and development. By recognizing their hard work and dedication, you are helping to build their confidence, self-esteem, and motivation to succeed. So take the time to acknowledge and celebrate your child's accomplishments, no matter how big or small, and watch as they continue to thrive in school and beyond.

Chapter 6:
Overcoming Common School Transition Challenges

Addressing separation anxiety and attachment issues during the school transition

Addressing separation anxiety and attachment issues during the school transition can be a challenging task for both parents and children. It is common for young children to experience feelings of anxiety and distress when faced with the prospect of being separated from their primary caregivers and entering a new environment such as school. However, with the right strategies and support in place, parents can help their children navigate this transition successfully.

One of the key ways to address separation anxiety and attachment issues during the school transition is to gradually introduce your child to the idea of separation. This can be done by starting with short periods of separation, such as leaving your child with a trusted caregiver or family member for short periods of time. By gradually increasing the length of time apart, your child can become more comfortable with the idea of being separated from you.

It is also important to establish a routine and set expectations for your child's time at school. By creating a predictable schedule and routine for drop-off and pick-up times, your child can feel more secure and know what to expect each day. Additionally, providing your child with a special item from home, such as a favorite toy or blanket, can provide comfort and a sense of familiarity during the school day.

Another helpful strategy for addressing separation anxiety and attachment issues during the school transition is to communicate openly and honestly with your child about their feelings. Encourage your child to express their emotions and validate their feelings of anxiety or fear. By acknowledging and validating your child's emotions, you can help them feel understood and supported as they navigate this challenging transition.

Finally, it is important for parents to practice self-care and seek support for themselves during this time of transition. Parenting a child through separation anxiety and attachment issues can be emotionally taxing, and it is important for parents to take care of themselves in order to be able to effectively support their child. Seeking out support from other parents, caregivers, or a mental health professional can provide valuable resources and guidance for navigating this challenging time. By implementing these strategies and seeking support when needed, parents can help their child successfully navigate separation anxiety and attachment issues during the school transition.

Dealing with peer pressure and social dynamics in the classroom

Navigating the playground can sometimes be harder for a child than learning to read. Social dynamics change rapidly, and the desire to fit in is incredibly powerful. Instead of just telling your child to "be yourself," give them the actual scripts they need to handle tricky situations. Role-play scenarios at home: "What could you say if someone tells you that you can't play with them?" or "How do you respond if a friend asks you to do something you know is against the rules?" Giving them a chance to practice these boundaries in the safety of your living room prepares them to stand their ground in the cafeteria.

One of the key ways to help your child deal with peer pressure in the classroom is to teach them how to assert themselves and set boundaries. Encourage your child to speak up for themselves and express their opinions and preferences. By doing so, your child will learn to stand up for themselves and resist negative peer influences.

It is also important to foster open communication with your child about their experiences in the classroom. Encourage them to share any concerns or difficulties they may be facing with their peers. By creating a safe space for your child to express themselves, you can provide them with the support they need to navigate through social challenges.

Furthermore, as a parent, it is important to model positive social behaviors for your child. Show them how to be respectful, empathetic, and inclusive towards others. By demonstrating these values in your own interactions, you can help your child develop healthy social skills and relationships in the classroom.

Overall, dealing with peer pressure and social dynamics in the classroom requires patience, understanding, and guidance from parents. By equipping your child with the tools and support they need to navigate through these challenges, you can help them build confidence, resilience, and positive social relationships in the classroom.

Supporting your child through academic challenges and learning differences

Supporting your child through academic challenges and learning differences can be a challenging aspect of parenting, but it is crucial for their success in school. As a parent, it is important to recognize and address any academic challenges or learning differences that your child may be facing. By being proactive and providing the necessary support, you can help your child overcome these obstacles and thrive in the classroom.

One of the first steps in supporting your child through academic challenges is to identify the specific areas where they may be struggling. This may involve observing their behavior in the classroom, talking to their teachers, or seeking the advice of a learning specialist. Once you have a better understanding of your child's academic challenges, you can work with their teachers and school administrators to develop a plan to address these issues.

It is also important to provide emotional support to your child during this time. Academic challenges and learning differences can be frustrating and stressful for children, and they may need extra reassurance and encouragement from their parents. By being patient, understanding, and supportive, you can help your child build confidence and resilience as they navigate through their academic struggles.

Parenting strategies for easing school transition can also play a crucial role in supporting your child through academic challenges and learning differences.

By creating a positive and nurturing environment at home, you can help your child feel more confident and prepared for the challenges they may face in school. Encouraging open communication, setting realistic expectations, and providing consistent support can all help your child feel more comfortable and secure as they navigate through their academic journey.

In conclusion, supporting your child through academic challenges and learning differences is an important aspect of parenting that can have a significant impact on their success in school. By being proactive, providing emotional support, and implementing effective parenting strategies, you can help your child overcome obstacles and thrive academically. Remember that every child is unique, and it may take time to find the right approach that works best for your child. With patience, understanding, and perseverance, you can help your child achieve their full potential in the classroom.

Chapter 7: Celebrating Success and Milestones

Reflecting on your child's growth and development since starting school

As a parent, one of the most rewarding experiences is watching your child grow and develop over time. Starting school marks a significant milestone in your child's life, and it's important to take a moment to reflect on their growth and development since beginning this new chapter. Reflecting on your child's progress can help you gain valuable insights into their strengths, challenges, and overall well-being.

Since starting school, you may have noticed significant changes in your child's behavior, social skills, and academic abilities. Take some time to think about how your child has adapted to the school environment, made new friends, and learned new skills. Reflecting on these changes can help you appreciate the progress your child has made and identify areas where they may need additional support or encouragement.

It's also important to consider your child's emotional well-being since starting school. Starting school can be a challenging and emotional time for children, as they navigate new experiences, routines, and expectations. Reflect on how your child has been coping with the transition and whether they have been displaying any signs of stress, anxiety, or difficulty adjusting. By reflecting on your child's emotional well-being, you can better understand their needs and provide the necessary support and reassurance.

Parenting strategies play a crucial role in easing the school transition for your child. Reflect on the strategies you have implemented to support your child's adjustment to school, such as establishing routines, maintaining open communication, and fostering a positive and supportive home environment.

Consider the effectiveness of these strategies and whether there are any additional steps you can take to further support your child's growth and development.

In conclusion, reflecting on your child's growth and development since starting school can provide valuable insights into their progress, emotional well-being, and overall well-being. By taking the time to reflect on your child's journey, you can better understand their needs, strengths, and challenges, and make informed decisions to support their successful school transition. Remember that every child is unique, and it's important to celebrate their individual achievements and milestones along the way.

Setting goals for the future and supporting your child's continued academic success

Setting goals for the future and supporting your child's continued academic success are crucial aspects of parenting that can make a significant impact on your child's school transition. As parents, it is important to help your child set realistic and achievable goals for their academic journey. Encouraging your child to have a vision for their future can motivate them to strive for success and stay focused on their studies.

One way to support your child's academic success is to establish a routine that includes dedicated time for homework, studying, and extracurricular activities. By creating a structured environment at home, you can help your child develop good study habits and time management skills that will benefit them in school and beyond. Setting aside specific times for homework and study sessions can also help your child stay organized and on track with their academic responsibilities.

In addition to setting goals and establishing a routine, it is important to communicate openly with your child about their academic progress and challenges. By being actively involved in your child's education, you can provide the necessary support and guidance to help them overcome obstacles and reach their full potential. This may involve attending parent-teacher conferences, reviewing report cards together, and discussing any concerns or issues that may arise.

Another effective way to support your child's academic success is to encourage a growth mindset.

Instead of focusing solely on grades and achievements, emphasize the importance of effort, perseverance, and learning from mistakes. By fostering a positive attitude towards challenges and setbacks, you can help your child develop resilience and a strong work ethic that will serve them well throughout their academic journey.

In conclusion, setting goals for the future and supporting your child's continued academic success are essential components of parenting that can have a lasting impact on your child's school transition. By creating a supportive and structured environment at home, communicating openly about academic progress, and fostering a growth mindset, you can help your child thrive in school and achieve their full potential. Remember that every child is unique, so it is important to tailor your parenting strategies to meet your child's individual needs and abilities.

Recognizing the importance of ongoing communication and support in your child's school journey

Recognizing the importance of ongoing communication and support in your child's school journey is crucial for their success and well-being. As parents, it is important to stay connected with your child's school and teachers to ensure that they are receiving the support they need. By establishing open lines of communication, you can stay informed about your child's progress, address any concerns or challenges they may be facing, and work together with teachers to create a positive learning environment for your child.

One of the key aspects of ongoing communication is building a strong partnership with your child's teachers. By establishing a collaborative relationship with teachers, you can gain valuable insights into your child's academic and social development. This partnership allows you to work together to address any issues that may arise, develop strategies to support your child's learning, and ensure that they are thriving in the classroom environment. By staying connected with teachers, you can also stay informed about upcoming events, projects, and assignments, allowing you to support your child in their school journey.

In addition to communicating with teachers, it is important to also maintain open lines of communication with your child. By engaging in regular conversations with your child about their school experiences, you can gain valuable insights into their thoughts, feelings, and concerns. This communication allows you to provide emotional support, address any anxieties or worries they may have, and offer guidance and reassurance as they navigate the challenges of school. By fostering a strong relationship with your child based on trust and open communication, you can help them feel supported and empowered in their school journey.

Another important aspect of ongoing communication and support is staying informed about school policies, procedures, and resources. By familiarizing yourself with the school's expectations and guidelines, you can ensure that your child is meeting academic requirements, following school rules, and accessing the support they need. Additionally, by staying informed about school resources such as counseling services, academic support programs, and extracurricular activities, you can help your child take advantage of opportunities for growth and enrichment. By being proactive and informed, you can ensure that your child is receiving the support they need to succeed in school.

In conclusion, recognizing the importance of ongoing communication and support in your child's school journey is essential for their academic success and emotional well-being. By building strong partnerships with teachers, maintaining open lines of communication with your child, and staying informed about school policies and resources, you can create a supportive and positive learning environment for your child. By actively engaging in your child's school journey and providing the necessary support and guidance, you can help them thrive academically and emotionally as they navigate the challenges of school.